10 Critical Strategies
for Finding Fulfillment
in a Hectic World

10 Critical Strategies for Finding Fulfillment in a Hectic World

Julie O'Keeffe, ACC

authorHOUSE®

AuthorHouse™
1663 Liberty Drive
Bloomington, IN 47403
www.authorhouse.com
Phone: 1-800-839-8640

First published by AuthorHouse 6/02/2011

ISBN: 978-1-4567-5625-3 (e)
ISBN: 978-1-4567-5626-0 (sc)

Library of Congress Control Number: 2011904872

Printed in the United States of America

Registered trademarks: Weight Watchers®, Teflon®, Frisbee®, Pop-Tarts®

Certain stock imagery © Thinkstock.

This book is printed on acid-free paper.

Don't Wait for Someday.

It
Never
Arrives.

Contents

Foreword

This book is about fulfillment, specifically living *fully* in today's world. Many of us are plugged in, turned on, and captive to schedules and "to do" lists. When we look at the amount of personal energy we expend, it's a wonder the earth doesn't shake on its axis as we collectively collapse at the end of the day.

Our collective and individual spirits often rise to the occasion. At other times, the body sends up a flare, in the form of high blood pressure, illness, or anxiety, to notify us that we need to slow down. This *slowing down* process involves learning a new way of operating, a new way of *being* in the world. It consists of an emotional, spiritual, and physical transition into a new space. The process even includes changes in the brain, where the chemicals and hormones related to stress dissipate and leave space for those related to happiness.

Over the course of 35 years, as a wellness coach, psychotherapist, and Buddhist chaplain, I have seen the ability for wellness strategies and healthy practices to permanently and dramatically increase an individual's quality of life. When a person embarks on the change process, they are able to reclaim and reinvent their lives.

Julie serves as an example of someone with a strong desire to work in partnership with others to restore their health and happiness. I met Julie years ago in an international 31 week coaching class I teach. She was hard to miss that first morning in our teleconference classroom. Why? Because it's rare to find a woman who synthesizes what life gives her, breathes into it and then lives and shares her inner wisdom. That morning she unselfishly revealed her caring and generous heart, sharp wit, and curious brain. Julie radiated wellness!

In a world where "I am so overwhelmed" is the default answer to "How are you?" Julie is a breath of fresh air for clients and organizations who are ready to take the next steps in living the ten critical strategies outlined in this book.

Are you ready to step away from your habituated, monochromatic living into a world that is alive and emerging once again? Yes? Then I challenge you to step away from your "to do" list and replace it with Julie's book. Fully participate in the exercises. Cultivate the strategies.

Remember, this is *your* life.

With a deep bow to you and all that you contribute,

Ann-Marie McKelvey, LPCC, MCC
Buddhist Chaplain, Coach and Psychotherapist
www.AnnMarieMcKelvey.com
www.AnnMariesGallery.com

Preface

Wellness is a term we hear frequently these days. It seems there's an acupuncturist on every corner, an employee wellness program in every company, and a yoga mat in every minivan. The health and wellness movement has swept the country and matured into its own industry. Considering that a majority of Americans smoked in the 50's and Frank Shorter only popularized running in the 70's, we have made major strides in becoming a society of keen health awareness.

We are also a society of high stress. We expect more from ourselves than is realistic, are overwhelmed by our obligations, and choose lifestyles that are not conducive to rest. Our complicated lives have driven us to the edge of health. It remains to be seen whether the wellness movement can tackle the *sources* of our societal stress on a large scale. The tide *is* turning and if we can collectively develop new societal standards and allow ourselves to slow down, work fewer hours, worry less, and laugh more, we might just find the meaning and fulfillment we all want in life.

Fortunately, as individuals we do not need to wait for the societal tide to turn to start leading a more fulfilling life. We can each act now to strengthen our own emotional, psychological, spiritual, and physical health, on our own terms. Our time and decisions are under our control, more than we believe. If we choose, we can exercise our own power just a bit more each day to regain a healthy balance in our lives. Healthy living starts with a deeper awareness of our own needs and the ability to strategize how to act on those needs. A life coach, friend, or partner can help us focus on this process. The point is, we just need to start.

My Fun (-damental) Decision in 2001

In 2001, I was on my own stressful treadmill working fulltime, raising kids, and managing domestic life. I was deeply aware of my own lack of balance and the mild depression that accompanied it. Then I got a phone call from my friend Jan in Atlanta, unleashing a string of events. Below are the pivotal moments.

> January 15, 2001. *"Julie, you need to come down here and do a race with me. It's called a triathlon. I saw people doing it last week and it looks really cool. You just have to swim, bike, and run."*
>
> April 21, 2001. *I'm standing on the edge of an outdoor pool in Birmingham, Alabama, next to Jan, ready to literally dive into my first*

triathlon. I'm the only person from Wisconsin. I traveled a long way to try a new sport.

June 22, 2001. *I'm standing at the edge of Lake Wazeecha, outside Port Edwards, Wisconsin, next to Jan. It's the day before our second triathlon and a fit-looking gentleman in his seventies scans the lake with his eyes. We ask if he's doing the race and he says, "Yeah, I'm doing it with my son. He got me started doing triathlons back when I was in my early fifties and I've now knocked off over 100 races." I am overtaken with the magnitude of his achievement. As we walk away, I can't stop thinking about it.*

The following day. *The event has started and I'm struggling in the lake, trying to propel myself forward. This is an ice cube race. I have never subjected my body to such cold water in my life. My lungs are in shock and won't take in air. I don't own a wet suit and when I get out of the water, my arms are numb. All of these athletes are NUTS!*

And yet, the idea of creating a long-term fitness goal took hold of me that weekend. One hundred races. I would be healthy long into the future.

At the time, my son, David, was four and my daughter, Heather, was seven. I had moved to Wisconsin where I faced the risk of packing on weight from cheese, beer, and long winters. I dreaded the thought of turning into a butterball, so a long-term fitness goal seemed like an excellent preventative measure. Knowing I'd be vibrant and able to enjoy life far down the road was also extremely enticing.

> *100 triathlons. I run some scenarios through my head. What if I aim for 100 races in 25 years? That would be four each year. Or maybe in 20 years, with five each year. I'd be 54 years old when I reach 100.*

> *"Jan, that guy on the beach yesterday really impressed me. What a great way to stay in shape. Don't laugh, but I think I could do 100 races, too! Can you just imagine? Maybe I could do five a year for 20 years."*

Ten years have now elapsed since I set that goal in 2001 and during that time I have completed 50 races! The landscape of my life has changed dramatically over the same period. I've gotten divorced, completed a half Ironman triathlon, climbed Mt. Kilimanjaro, changed careers twice, started my own business, bought a new house, and enjoyed dozens of new friendships. I have led my kids backpacking 40 miles through the Grand Canyon. I also met Michael, my true soul mate.

Life is busy and there have been times when I've thought about leaving the goal behind me in order to pursue other things or just free up time for other weekend events. But in the winter, when I'm confined to the house and instinctively eating fat-producing carbs to keep warm, I remember the important role that the annual cycle of races plays in my life. The sport of triathlon helps me gauge my level of fitness over the years. It allows me to surround myself with people who share my enthusiasm for outdoor activity. It also helps me keep my value around health and wellness at the front of my mind.

> Fall **2020**. *It's 7 a.m. and I'm standing ankle deep in a lake, next to Jan, poised for a start gun to go off. My kids, now 24 and 27, and Michael are spectating from the side of the beach. They've used a thick marker to write "Happy 100th race, Mom" on the back of my leg. Jan trash talks in her most innocuous voice, "I'll wait for you at the finish line," to which I retort, "In your wildest dreams!"*

It's Your Turn

What's vitally important in your own life? Is it your health, friends, family, romance, career, intellectual challenge? Whatever it may be, make sure you devote enough time and energy to it. Attach time-bound goals and develop strategies to get there. Learn to remove obstacles that stand in your way. And finally, create a circle of supporters who will get you through the rough patches and celebrate your achievements and growth.

We are most fulfilled when we pursue our most cherished needs, goals, and wishes. Don't wait. "Someday" never comes. Just start dabbling in whatever would make you happy and see what happens.

You might love the outcome.

Acknowledgements

Ann Marie McKelvey, thank you for your humor, encouragement, and wisdom as I found my footing and voice as a life coach. You truly helped launch my new trajectory and I hope I bring the same energy and support to others that you have brought to me.

Thank you Mom and Dad, for believing in me. Your unconditional support has meant a lot.

Michael, you are full of wisdom, patience, and love. Thank you for offering all of them. Your coming into my life has made all the difference.

Heather and David, I know you think the little inspirational sayings taped to the wall by the back door are goofy and at the same time I see you living out those virtues, values, and beliefs. I'm very proud of you. Thanks for keeping it real.

Paul and Tiffany, your kindness and generosity have meant a lot to me over the years.

Introduction

Does your daily life reflect what is truly important to you? Our day-to-day activities can sometimes push aside the larger picture of our life. We tend to get caught up in things such as our workload, kid activities, unfinished laundry, and unpaid bills. It's important to step back and evaluate where you are today. Is your life where you want it to be right now?

Some of us lose sight of our values and goals and unknowingly wander off our desired path. Likewise, some of us are quite aware when we change our path whether it's to raise children, take care of an ailing parent, or adapt to some other life-changing event. For others of us, we may be on the right path but not moving forward; instead, we're caught in a well-worn groove that we've created.

What if you were told that you could reclaim your life, gain control, and get out of your rut? Let me tell you that you can, and you will, find fulfillment with the help of these time-tested strategies. You will feel empowered as you apply techniques that are sure to help you rediscover yourself, rekindle a buried passion, and push through an impasse to get you moving forward.

When traveling, we rely on navigational tools to help us get from place to place. Consider this book a tool for navigating your unique path in life. These strategies will help you set and follow your internal compass, explore new roads, and embrace all your experiences along the way.

If you feel both excited and anxious about the prospect of leading the life you want and deserve, take it in stride. Anxiety is a natural part of our emotional response to possible change, even when those changes lead to greater fulfillment. This book will help turn that nervous energy into forward momentum.

This is your life—take hold and live it on your terms.

Ready? Let's get started.

Be Resourceful in Balancing Priorities

Sometimes it seems like we only have time to focus on one or two priorities, so we attend to them at the expense of others. Neglecting priorities almost always catches up with us and we end up spending more time dealing with the consequences than the initial issue would have required.

Life would be better if we just had more control, right? The fact is, there are often more options than we realize. It might only take a bit of creativity and a fresh perspective to discover the choices that are actually within our control.

Outrageous brainstorming and resourcefulness

To break through your sense of being "locked up" by your life, try a technique with a friend called outrageous brainstorming. The strategy consists of two steps. First, come up with crazy, off-the-wall ways to solve a problem. The more unrealistic or impractical, the better. The point is to go so far outside reasonable boundaries that the real boundaries don't seem so immovable. Doing this breaks the tension and allows you to see your circumstances with a fresh perspective.

Say you'd like to start a running routine in the morning but it interferes with rousing your seven- and nine-year old kids from bed and helping them get breakfast. Maybe you hire Rachael Ray to cook breakfast. Or, you send your kids to the neighbor's house to steal food off the table. Or, you give the kids diet pills to suppress their appetite. You get the idea.

Secondly, take a more practical look at your present circumstances. View the situation from every angle. Consider assumptions that might be false. Remove these assumptions just for a minute and see what possibilities surface. Consider resources that might be available to you. Your new frame of mind will allow you to think more expansively and with a greater sense of empowerment.

With the example above, maybe the kids could help you cut up fruit every night to grab from the fridge in the morning. You could move the microwave within arm's reach so they can heat up their own oatmeal. You could offer the nine-year-old a movie rental once a week if she will supervise breakfast. To get the kids out of bed, perhaps they are old enough to take some responsibility for this task, too. Let them each pick out a fun alarm clock at the store and practice using it for a week. Then let them go solo.

We often overestimate our own importance and need for involvement. We can't imagine certain tasks without our presence. Well, imagine it! Imagine the freedom it brings and the healthy changes that can result, not just for you, but often for others as well. Consider how your children might grow from the new challenge and achieve a greater sense of self-sufficiency and skill mastery.

Apply it to your life

The next time you're with a friend, ask her to help you do some outrageous brainstorming around a priority that has slipped off the radar. Let go of the wrinkle-causing worry for a minute and just have fun. Break free of the tension, look at the situation with fresh eyes, and give yourself permission to solve the problem.

Then implement the solution, without guilt! Explain to individuals who might be impacted the reason for the change and the importance of trying the new approach. Explain how they might benefit.

Model the behavior of someone who wants to live their best life! And be that person!

$\mathcal{P}$ut Your Fears Aside

How many of life's decisions have you made based on fear and your need for certainty? You might gain peace of mind by knowing exactly what will happen but on the flip side, it's also very limiting. It's possible to squeeze more out of life and still feel some sense of safety. It's a two-step process: testing your limits and recalibrating.

Test your limits

Each of us has a natural balancing point between safety and risk. You might be willing to jump from a three-foot ledge but not a six-foot ledge. Somewhere between three feet and six feet is the tipping point, the point at which you are uncomfortable taking the risk.

So first, test your limits. It will allow you to locate the tipping point. Do you want to try jumping from four feet? Or perhaps start with three feet six inches and work your way up. You see, you can find your limits any way you want. It's usually not an "all or nothing" proposition. Just try a little of what you believe makes you nervous and test it.

By testing your limits, you might learn that you are capable of more than you think. Not surprising, right? Yet we all go through life making assumptions about our limits, forcing tight boundaries around us that are unnecessary. Loosen up these boundaries and you have more room to breathe. More room to be curious. More room to grow.

Recalibrate

Second, recalibrate. With this process, you move the tipping point. If you continue to jump just a little beyond your comfort zone each time, you will feel more and more comfortable with every jump. Before you know it, it will require a greater height to make you feel uneasy. That's recalibrating.

We recalibrate in life all the time. We change our concept of our ideal weight as we move from youth to age 20, 30, and 40. We change our concept of quality, such that the "expensive" watch we bought at age 10 with our allowance may not seem so cool at age 16. We adjust to life's changing framework.

Impact

If you've ever been around successful individuals who seem immune to problems that would be difficult for rest of us, that immunity is simply each person's recalibration in action. Their definition of what constitutes a problem has evolved over time as they've exposed themselves to more challenging situations. They can handle more, because it doesn't feel overwhelming. They have adjusted.

Your fears

What is the next big decision you want to make in your life? Look at the options available to you and identify the fears and risks that you associate with each one. You can't always jump off a ledge to test your limits, so perhaps sit down with a pencil and paper and jot down some thoughts about each option. See if you can find your tipping point, being completely honest with yourself, rather than making general assumptions about your capability. Then check whether any of your options become more possible and less frightening.

Now, still looking at the options available to you, consider a way to engage in one or more activities that seem a bit risky or make you uncomfortable. Go beyond that need for certainty and explore just a bit. That means going to a Weight Watchers® meeting despite embarrassment, attending the neighborhood book club meeting despite a lack of acquaintances, and asking someone out on a date despite fear of rejection. If you survive the first time, try it a second time. Then a third. Focus on the aspects of the activity that are pleasurable. This will allow you to build up some tolerance for the uncomfortable part and soon you may find that you have recalibrated and can actually enjoy yourself due to your new perspective. What was hard becomes easy. What was scary begins to feel safe.

So get over yourself already

Fear is all about not knowing what is going to happen. Success is all about embracing uncertainty and learning to feel safe in the process.

What fears are you ready to put aside? Start now and experience a fuller life with more fun and adventure along the way. Don't miss out!

Update Your Identity to Reflect Your Current Capabilities

How do you describe yourself? Some labels are easy, such as mother, employee, student, or accountant. But how else do you define yourself and does it help or hinder you?

Your identity may be set in the past, based on old assumptions of yourself. Do you still fit that mold or have you changed? Can you still run 400 meters in 55 seconds? Do you still tell bad jokes? Does a statement like "I'm happiest when surrounded by x or y" still ring true? Does a past relationship still limit your belief about what you have to offer?

The "truths" we carry around

Our sense of identity is largely defined by where we've been. We've been shaped into who we are today by the roads we've traveled down in our lives, the people and events along the way, and the conclusions we've drawn from each experience.

Let's say when you were 10, you walked into a gas station with a friend, only to have the attendant make some bigoted remark. It may not have affected you, but it may have gnawed at your friend. Her story, her sense of who she is, may now include that incident and the "truth" that she took away from the experience. Her truth might be that gas station attendants are uncaring, that it's important to take the high road, that she herself is undeserving, or that bigotry is dangerous. If she chooses to incorporate any of these truths into her life's story, it shapes her identity.

Rework your story

We actually have choices when it comes to which events and people we allow to contribute to our identity. We each have millions of experiences in our past. Which experiences and truths have you kept with you? What if you were to take a box full of all your experiences, dump them on the floor, and then sort through the pile and choose a different combination of people, events, conclusions, and truths? Perhaps you'd de-emphasize some of the awkward moments in your life and highlight some proud moments that had faded in your memory.

It's your coloring book and you get to pick the crayons. Who are you, really? How strong are you? What are you capable of? What are you proud of? When do you dance and slide across the floor in your socks and underwear? What do you value most about yourself?

Embrace Versions 2.0, 3.0, 4.0

You get to choose your identity. Don't get stuck in the past. It doesn't matter what your parents think, how you've failed, or what went wrong. Cast aside outdated beliefs, old guilt, and negative labels. Who are you today? You get to choose.

Develop Your Resiliency

What's the difference between resiliency and Teflon®? Teflon doesn't let anything penetrate. Resiliency develops as a result of the penetration.

Resiliency is the ability to withstand the heartaches of life. It's moving through a traumatic period, surviving death, divorce, job loss, and all the disappointments that can throw us off kilter.

Resiliency manifests itself as strength of character. The most durable camping gear I own has been put to the test under a variety of conditions. The material is worn but the seams are strong. The most durable people I know have overcome tremendous obstacles thrown in their path. They have scars, but their integrity is rock solid.

I have a friend who broke his nose playing basketball not once, but twice, many years ago. He asked me whether I thought he should get it fixed. I said, "Of course not. It defines your whole face." Something about that crooked nose conveys to me his ability to surface after a struggle, embrace insights, and gracefully move on. Having his nose straightened would somehow remove an outward testament to his experience and resiliency.

Three ways to get there

How can we each develop resiliency? Here are a few ideas. Try to do them as often as possible.

Let things stick. Be the opposite of Teflon. Allow yourself to experience the highs and lows of life. It's only when we embrace our emotions that we can learn from them. Sweeping things under the rug and pushing emotions aside may seem like a good coping mechanism, but it's unhealthy and leads to stress-related illness and depression.

Show compassion. Lighten the load by approaching situations with compassion. If someone seems to be making your life difficult, look for a positive, universal truth related to human behavior. For example, imagine how John may have been hurt during his divorce. Perhaps that is the cause of his anger now. Imagine how Sarah may have cared for her mother during her decline. Perhaps that is the cause of her resistance to change now.

We all want the same things out of life. It's just that we each get a little jostled along the way and our gears can get out of sync. Compassion helps us appreciate the universality of struggle and strength of human spirit. It's the awareness you need to build resiliency.

Be willing to fail. It's natural to be disappointed from past failures and our inability to solve a particular problem. Accept failure as the opportunity to grow. If a one-year-old child were to give up after stumbling through her first steps, she'd never learn to walk. Each step is a small win. As adults, each of our "failed" relationships is a small win, each marathon we don't complete, each job we leave, each rejected grant proposal. We learn from all of them. Pick yourself up, dust yourself off, and move on.

Don't wait any longer

Resiliency is about acceptance, insight, and action. About recognizing the good stuff sitting right in front of us, despite wounds still healing.

So look up. Look up, scan the horizon, and take the next step forward.

$\mathcal{D}$o the Fun Things in Life Now

You may have heard of the movie *The Bucket List* with Morgan Freeman and Jack Nicholson, where two terminally-ill men escape from a cancer ward and head off on a road trip with a wish list of to-dos before they die.

So really, do we need to wait that long, until it's almost too late, to go after all the things we dream about?

Have you always wanted to visit India? Or the Grand Canyon? Or take scuba diving lessons? Or plan a reunion with all your cousins back at the lake where you used to spend your summers?

Here's my suggestion: do it now.

Remove Obstacles

Write down the barriers that stand in your way: money, time, lack of a partner to do an activity with, a possible relocation, parenting responsibilities . . . Then get creative about removing or managing the barriers.

Make the time. Admit it, you can make time when you need to. If you've ever had surgery and spent time recovering, you know that matters can either wait or someone else can take care of them. That means you can take that trip to India without your world falling apart back home.

Ease up on the requirements. Consider which parts of your desired experience are essential and which you can jettison. You may be waiting on pieces of the puzzle that are unnecessary. Remove those variables from the equation and your goal may be easier than you think. When I wanted to climb Mt. Kilimanjaro, I couldn't find anyone to go with me. I finally concluded I could manage on my own. And I did!

Be flexible. Allow for some latitude in the experience itself. Don't become irrationally attached to a specific plan. When I found the opportunity to go hiking in New Zealand, it was too late to book hut-to-hut lodging along my preferred route. I ended up on another trail just as nice.

Make financial trade-offs or save up. There's no way around the money issue. You'll need to find it somewhere. Perhaps it's more important to follow your passion than remodel the bathroom. Research shows that money makes us happier if we spend it on experiences and other people, not gadgets and fast cars. What can you live without?

Stop wavering and buy the ticket. If your trip includes air travel, go online, find some flights, and click on "purchase now." Your hands might get sweaty, you might need to walk around the kitchen or gulp down some wine, but come back, sit down, and take the leap. With the opportunity for indecision behind you, you can start to get excited and enjoy the anticipation.

Finally, for some of you out there who might feel guilt, give up on the idea that you need to "earn" your experience. Start believing that you have one life—this one chance to soak up all the sunsets and margaritas you can!

So are you ready to live a little? Start the conversations and make the phone calls needed to get moving. Figure out the steps involved and tackle them one by one. Don't stop until you hear someone announcing "Please fasten your seat belts."

Get Real about Your Goals

You come home from work, plop down on the couch, and this fleeting thought runs through your head, so fast you're barely conscious of it: "If things were different I would be _____." Insert your own desire here.

Over the years the voice of your desires has faded like a cherished European train ticket stub from college days. Yeah, back in the day when life was easy. Well, the truth is it wasn't easy, we just worked harder on our desires!

So here's a new, stronger voice: Get real about your goals. And by that I mean: Make your planning and preparation real. Combine your thoughts with actions. Here's a few ways to do it.

Go public. Proclaiming your goal to everyone is a great way to propel yourself into action. We like to honor our commitments and when we publicly announce our intention, we gain a real sense of ownership. When the goal is only in our head, we are less accountable and it becomes fairly easy to fall back on Plan B, the status quo.

Along with sharing your goal with others, don't be shy about letting each person know how he or she can help. If you request a specific action from each person, you can build a team that will help you rally when you need it most.

Make trade-offs to carve out the needed time. This is the real stickler. We tend to fall into routines and yield to daily urgencies and obligations so easily that we do not carve out time for our neglected goals. Schedule some time several days a week to complete tasks related to your goal. Be adamant with yourself about sticking to the schedule.

Again, louder: Be adamant with yourself about sticking to the schedule. Way too many people remark, Well, such-and-such happened on Monday. Tuesday was bowling night. Wednesday my daughter had a recital. Thursday I was too tired and Friday I ran errands. We could rattle that stuff off until the end of time. Choose and commit. And of course, get back on the horse when things go awry.

Make a vision board. A vision board uses images to illustrate your desired outcome. You can start with an 8x11 sheet of paper or a 24x36 poster board. Sidebar: If you're groaning over the idea of an arts and crafts project, don't worry, I get it. Trust me—this truly works! Add any images or words that clearly represent your goal and what life will be like when you achieve it.

Place the vision board in a prominent place in your home. Obnoxiously. Family and friends will see that you are serious about your efforts and when they rib you about it, know they are impressed you're working towards something that brings personal fulfillment!

Work on your goal urgently. Lean into it with a specific action every day. Let others help you succeed and when you do, include them in the celebration!

Take a Second Look at Obstacles

Internal and external obstacles can stop you cold when you're trying to change. You become resigned to their apparent permanence. The obstacles grow and grow in your mind.

What's the reality of the external environment and your inner beliefs? How can you view your situation as a challenge rather than certain defeat? If you change the way you think about both the obstacles that block your path and your own ability to tackle them, you will feel more empowered to address your situation. Here are three ways to change your approach.

Remind yourself of past successes and the personal strengths you applied. We tend to minimize past experiences when we have successfully navigated obstacles. Think back on times that you dealt well with a difficult situation. What did you do that you're not yet doing now? Perhaps you had the courage to face a problem squarely, the social intelligence to connect with others who could help, or the creativity to look at options not readily apparent. You can apply that courage, social intelligence, creativity, or a host of other innate abilities to your current situation.

Most of us use specific personal strengths over and over and over again. If you're not sure what your strengths are, try taking a character strength survey from the VIA Institute on Character, available for free online. It will let you know your top five strengths from a list of 24 strengths that psychologists have identified through extensive research. Life coaches use the survey with their clients to help them get the most out of the strengths they possess.

Question your assumptions. What are your beliefs about the obstacle currently in your path? Can you know for sure that these beliefs are true? How much evidence can you provide and is that evidence exaggerated to any degree? If you find yourself using the words "always" and "never" when you cite evidence, you may be discounting possibilities or underestimating situations and people. Life is dynamic and what was true yesterday or last year may not be true today. Often assumptions also serve to protect us from acknowledging our own accountability in moving forward. We can be our worst enemy in "staying stuck." It may be time to become your best friend.

Be childlike in your curiosity. As children, we are not yet jaded or resigned to anything. Be like that again. Get curious about strategies that might kick an obstacle to the curb. Ask yourself questions like, "I wonder how x might turn out if I try the y approach?", "I wonder if I can sustain...", or "What would happen if I..." Research by psychologist Todd Kashdan shows that curiosity is fundamental to inviting change and growth into our lives. Curiosity is the prelude to action.

What would your life look like if obstacles didn't stand in your way? Foster awareness into how you perceive obstacles and your own abilities. Once you take away the power of obstacles by changing your perspective, you are well on your way to clearing them from your path.

$\mathcal{P}$ut Your Values into Action

It's easy for our daily lives to be disconnected from our values.

- Do you value quality family time, yet spend lots of time at work?

- Do you value romance, yet spend little time seeking out a potential boyfriend/girlfriend or going out with the partner already in your life?

- Do you value healthy eating, yet eat a plate full of French fries at lunch?

We sometimes need reminding that we can't get what we don't seek out! It's up to each of us to take a long-term view and create a life that resonates with our values and promotes a sense of fulfillment. Try these three practices.

Make a list of your values, tape it to your bedroom mirror, and look at it every morning. Perhaps the easiest way to make your list is to start by thinking of times in your life when you've really enjoyed yourself. What were you doing? Who were you with? How did if feel? Jot down the top four or five events or situations. Your most important values are present in these situations and you can often see them more easily than if you just try to conceptualize a list. This process also helps avoid coming up with values like love, peace, and an end to world hunger, when it should be more specific to your own life.

Stick the list up where you'll see it every morning. Then ask yourself what you can do that day to honor at least two of your most important values.

Commit, schedule ahead, and don't cancel. If you want to make a real commitment to live according to your values, plan out for the entire week ahead how you will make time for a few activities that honor your values. Put the activities in your daily planner, with a block of appointed time, and confer with other people if you need to get others on board. They'll appreciate that someone else initiated an activity that resonates with their values, too. Then, don't cancel the activity just because you run out of milk, the dog needs a flee collar, or you get a phone call. We often put our own priorities behind any ol' urgent thing that comes up. Hello!

Create a personal action statement. Compose a statement that demonstrates how you put your values into action. It will help you own your values, enhance your sense of purpose, and get more engaged.

Write the verb tenses so that it sounds as if you're living out your values now, even if you're not quite there yet. For example, if you highly value socializing with friends but could use more money to support going out to eat with them, avoid using "I will have an income that supports a healthy social life" and write "My income supports a healthy social life" instead. Keep the length between 150 and 250 words.

My most important values are adventure, risk, creativity, tolerance, physical health, being outdoors, and quality time with friends and family. Here's my personal statement:

- I am a poster child for energy, action, warmth, and engagement.

- I use mountain bikes, skis, and Frisbees® to unite kindred spirits.

- National and state parks are a gift from past visionaries and I explore them with friends and family.

- My children sustain me with their humor and I actively support their development.

- I design and lead outdoor adventures where risk-taking and challenging activities enhance people's confidence, worldview, and faith in others.

- My active coaching practice helps others restore and strengthen their courage and faith.

- I honor my need for sun in winter by headin' south each January.

- My income supports a healthy social life and allows me the freedom to use my time as I see fit.

- I celebrate my partner with active support and encouragement and he supports my need for adventure.

- I am authentic. I love easily and forgive freely.

Take time to live your life the way you most desire! As long as you are pursuing that life, in harmony with your values, you'll be able to weather the bad days and utterly relish in the good ones!

Walk Over Boundaries

I know of a person in the South who won't drive her car for more than a couple of hours by herself. She feels she lacks the capacity as an adult woman. It seems to be based on traditional southern cultural norms around male and female roles.

My friend in Arizona, on the other hand, drives herself three hours to the nearest airport, my sister and I have each traveled alone to Africa, and a sixteen-year-old girl just sailed solo for four months around much of the world.

So let's talk boundaries! Ask yourself these questions:

1. What boundaries are holding me back?

2. Are they self-imposed or culturally-imposed?

3. Does anybody really care what I do?

4. What if I walked over the boundaries?

Boundaries can be a good thing, particularly with speed limits, murder laws, and required immunizations. It's best not to drive too fast, kill anyone, or forget to immunize your child.

On the other hand, what about wearing white after Labor Day? Or pulling your 13-year-old out of school for a week to go hiking in the Grand Canyon?

It's time to walk over unnecessary boundaries! Bust through them so that you can get on with your life. Let's break it down.

Examine the belief embedded in the boundary. Who invented this boundary and what is their belief? A handful of our forefathers created a constitutional boundary (i.e., document) incorporating a belief in the separation of church and state. That's cool. They also didn't believe everyone had the right to vote. Not so cool. You might only allow your child to take the car if they are back by 11 p.m., based on the belief that too much mischief happens late at night. That's probably good. But you might deny yourself a fun weekend getaway, based on the belief that your family cannot manage without you. That's probably not good.

Ask yourself whether the boundary has changed over time. Did your parents go to all of your junior high basketball games or tennis matches? What's your expectation with your own kids? Is there an engaging activity you'd like to try if you didn't feel obligated to adhere to culturally-prescribed roles as a parent?

Consider to what extent the important people in your life observe the same boundary. Some protestants in specific

Midwest towns won't mow their lawn on Sunday for religious reasons. Such practices only fall by the wayside if groups no longer value them. How would others view you if you change your behavior around common, unquestioned practices? Will the important people in your life embrace your decision? Can you gain their support if you value it?

Here's what I say: Ask the guy/gal out. Set an unrealistic goal. Sell the house, quit the job, and go get your Ph.D. Laugh too loud. Drive all night. Hitchhike to Alaska. Life is more fun when you ignore arbitrary boundaries and disregard limiting beliefs!

Expect Adversity in Your Adventures

When you think of adventure, what do you think of? Your daughter going off to college, remodeling your kitchen, or perhaps camping in the Rockies? You likely imagine some sort of event where you can't predict every detail of how the situation will play out. For example: What kind of friends will your daughter make her freshman year? Will there be unexpected issues in the kitchen walls when the contractor opens them up? What kind of weather will you have while camping?

When we plan something "big" and look forward to it for a long time, our expectations can become overly-heightened by all of the positives associated with the adventure. In real life, negatives are also along for the ride. In our day-to-day lives, we expect these challenges. If we run late for a meeting because of traffic, oh well. But when we get stuck in traffic and are late for our scuba diving lesson on vacation, it drives us nuts. If there are too many negatives that occur during our big event, it can put us in the dumps.

There are a few ways to keep adversity from steam-rolling over your adventure.

Expect problems. Set your sites on dealing with a handful of in-your-face problems. If you're with family or friends, keep in mind that individuals respond to adversity differently. Be prepared to help each other mentally process any serious situations that arise.

Laugh or cry. Let it out. I was once on vacation with my kids in Mexico when they were young. As the sole adult, I was trying to tackle a lot logistically. When we got to the front of a long line to get into a water park – our big event for the day – and my credit card didn't work for the second time, I had to go sit in a corner and have a little meltdown. React to and then release your stress so you can get on with your day.

Look forward. Look beyond the immediate situation to a point in time when the problem will no longer exist. Imagine relaxing in your beautiful, cozy new kitchen after all the contractors, noise, and dust are gone. This action will remind you that your current predicament is temporary and better times are ahead.

Take a break. If you become too overwhelmed with a predicament, take a break from your adventure. When it rains the entire week of your camping trip, get a hotel room one night and go to a great restaurant for dinner. Removing yourself from the immediate situation can let your emotional reserves return to their normal level, allowing you to put your coping skills back into normal use.

Get creative. Under stress, we often fail to think creatively or utilize resources that are available to us. My friend once took on the adventure of moving to a better neighborhood. When she ran out of money for moving expenses, it threw her for a loop. After taking a break and re-grouping, she realized that she didn't need to pay her professional moving crew to unload her belongings. She simply needed some strong people who would work for the bit of money she had left. She got the name of the local high school wrestling coach, called him, and three days later she had six wrestlers standing on her front porch, along with a coach holding donuts and orange juice!

You can come up with good solutions when you are able to take a few deep breaths in the midst of your adversity and engage in some creative brainstorming.

Your response to adversity while in full throttle adventure mode makes all the difference. While it might seem great to foresee and avoid misadventures, life would be too predictable and boring. It's the combination of expected and unexpected challenges that add up to produce lasting memories, great stories, and a sense of real accomplishment.

Bonus Strategy

Live in a Judgment-Free Zone

Several times a day, you may be in the habit of reflecting on your behavior, body, or decisions with self-criticism. It's common for us to put pressure on ourselves. The assumption is that there is a minimal personal standard that we must meet before we allow ourselves to relax.

What if you could wave a magic wand and just "Be Adequate" right at this moment? Let's say for a second that it's true, that during the current 24-hour period you meet all your standards in how you conduct yourself, how much you exercise, what you eat, and what you decide. That's great. However, the risk remains that tomorrow you might miss the mark. There's no certainty that you'll live up to your standard from day to day. In this way, each day starts with a question mark and you will either meet your standard or feel bad that you failed.

Here's an idea: Stop judging yourself. Stop measuring yourself against your adequacy standard. Instead, live in a judgment-free zone. This is a space where you may laugh and have fun without worry. Where you can express yourself freely and learn as you go. Where your natural intelligence and wisdom are obvious, your values are present, and your personality is authentic and appreciated.

Where is this sunny place in your life? It does exist, perhaps in some neglected state. Try these methods to inhabit it more frequently.

Remember you're human. Just like everyone else, you're flawed. You'll make mistakes as an employee, friend, parent, and partner. You'll eat a few too many cookies or waste a bit of time. Fortunately, the impact of your mistakes typically diminishes over time, fading from memory. So remember that you are human. Remember the times that, in spite of your flawed nature, you have met challenges in the face of obstacles. In that sense, you're actually quite remarkable in your abilities.

Practice loving kindness. Loving kindness is a Buddhist concept and form of unconditional love that can be cultivated through meditation. It involves showing compassion first towards oneself, then towards loved ones, friends, teachers, strangers, enemies, and finally towards all sentient beings. A person can resolve concerns about one's own self worth by beginning to see the inherent worth of all beings. Passing judgment on oneself or others becomes completely irrelevant.

Identify an unmet need. When you find that you are judging yourself, ask yourself what need is not being met at the moment. Notice any strong emotion that accompanies the need. You might feel angry because of an unmet need to be understood, lonely due to an unmet need for community, or scared because of an unmet need for security. Learn to identify your dominant emotion, uncover the need behind it, and explore ways to initiate filling that need. Try reading Marshall Rosenberg's *Non-Violent Communication: A Language for Life* to hone your skills in this area.

Replace anxiety with curiosity. You may become anxious when you try something new or become entangled in an uncomfortable situation. Rather than make judgments about the situation, try becoming curious about what might happen if you try a specific approach or action. For example, if you are in the midst of a tense discussion during a meeting at work, try asking yourself, "I wonder what would happen if I lower my voice when I speak?" or "I wonder how Jane will respond if I simply acknowledge her point of view more explicitly?" Becoming curious allows you to function a bit better in an unstable, unpredictable environment and try out new strategies without feeling vulnerable.

The act of judging requires energy. Anticipation of judgment can also hold your emotions hostage. Learn to live free of judgment and enjoy a renewed sense of spaciousness and freedom. You'll thrive in this sunny place.

About Coach Julie

Client Remarks

"Before working with you, I knew I had the ability to change, but was having a hard time achieving it. With your coaching I was able to understand on a deeper level what is important to me, what inspires me, and what I can do right now to make that real. I have renewed motivation to take action toward these goals and have developed a wellness plan that even my husband is now following!"

Sarah Johnson,
Kansas City, Kansas

"Thanks for all your coaching over the past eight months! You have been such a source of strength for me. I feel like I have my life back thanks to you."

Lynn Courtright,
Wakefield, Massachusetts

Attending to Cherished Goals—
And ready to help others find fulfillment

Cherished Needs, Goals, and Wishes

Julie is the kind of person who travels to Tanzania by herself to climb Africa's tallest mountain and who has a goal of completing 100 triathlons in 20 years. She believes that we all have the ability and time to take action on our most cherished goals, needs, and wishes—no matter where we're starting from. She leads by example and shares, "We have the power to make dramatic improvements in each area of our lives. Once we see that ability within ourselves, we can transform ourselves through big goals and small steps each day."

Scaling Mt. Kilimanjaro, Africa's tallest mountain

Julie's passion for empowering others and her ability to engage an audience make her a dynamic speaker and workshop leader. Her stories create learning moments and she presents powerful strategies and tools that can launch individuals further down their desired path.

Triathlon and Mentoring

Julie is an avid sprint triathlete and is on target to complete 100 races over a 20-year period. She is currently half way to her goal.

To help women from all walks of life achieve their fitness goals, Danskin hired Julie in 2009 to coordinate their triathlon mentor program. Leading up to the Chicago-area triathlon, 300 women gained skills, knowledge, and confidence to complete their first triathlon. Julie was at the finish line to congratulate each woman.

Iceland, Mops, and Hitchhiking

Julie's sense of adventure has taken her to every continent except Antarctica. She has completed a winter survival program in Norway, studied as a Fulbright Scholar in Iceland, mopped floors at a maternity hospital in Australia, ridden horses in Mongolia, summited Mt. Kilimanjaro in Africa, and scaled a volcano in South America. A 10-year marriage began with a honeymoon that involved hitchhiking 5400 miles to Alaska and back.

Julie currently spends her time coaching, parenting, working on an organic vegetable farm (and still eating Pop-Tarts®), and collecting camping gear. Her two teenage children pleasantly distract her and ignore her suggestions for personal development.

If you want to pick Julie's brain or a winning lottery ticket, use the following contact information:

Phone ~ 414.305.3113
Email ~ coachjulie@nextstepgoals.com

You can also find Julie in these locations:

Web ~ www.nextstepgoals.com
Twitter ~ @WhenIsSomeday
LinkedIn ~ www.linkedin.com/in/okeeffe
Facebook ~ www.facebook.com/julie.okeeffe1

Science, Life Experience, and Unique Paths

In her active coaching practice, Julie informs her work with the theory and empirical data emerging from a branch of psychology called *positive psychology*. The American Psychological Association forged this new path a decade ago with a goal of gaining scientific understanding of what makes people thrive.

Of course, individuals who work with Julie also fold their own wisdom and common sense into creating their personal development plans. Each person's life experience, core values, and strengths are raw materials that they weave together to design their future. Julie thrives on helping each individual chart their own unique path.

Julie is credentialed as an associate certified coach through the International Coach Federation (ICF). She graduated from an accredited coaching program and adheres to the ICF Code of Ethics in her practice. To learn more, visit the ICF web site at www.coachfederation.org.

Leading a group backpacking in the Grand Canyon

Hiking 42 miles with her kids